Anglesey Abbey Gardens

CAMBRIDGESHIRE

A souvenir guide

National Trust

A GREAT 20TH-CENTURY GARDEN

The gardens of Anglesey Abbey are one of the great garden creations of the 20th century.

The vision of one man, Huttleston Broughton, 1st Lord Fairhaven, the gardens were created between 1930 and his death in 1966, when they were given, with the house, to the National Trust. Covering an area of 114 acres (about 46 hectares), they are an oasis of garden splendour on the edge of the featureless Cambridgeshire Fenland.

The gardens are a series of compartments of varying size, each surrounded either by immaculately trimmed hedges or by informal tapestries of trees and shrubs, carefully linked by shaded pathways. A number of avenues give spectacular vistas where the eye is led to one of the many sculptures which adorn the garden.

The gardens continue to demonstrate the style and high standards initiated by the founder, while balancing the needs of visitors and wildlife alike. Environmentally friendly practices are promoted within the gardens, where pioneering methods of recycling, composting and mulching are employed to ensure that little goes to waste.

However, the prime function of the gardens is to give you pleasure, and I have no doubt they will do this in any season and for many generations to come. Enjoy your visit, as you see for yourself.

Above Lord Fairhaven on the South Lawn; painted by Alexander Christie in 1952

Left A Six-spot Burnet moth

Opposite The Coade stone caryatids on the Cross Avenue

A GARDEN FOR ALL SEASONS

Anglesey offers an abundance of interest throughout the whole year.

Above The Rose Garden in summer

Above right *Dahlia* 'Barbarry Pointer'

Spring
In spring, massed drifts of daffodils flourish throughout the gardens, while over 4000 hyacinths emerge in meticulously maintained formal flower beds.

Summer
Summer brings the spectacle of magnificent herbaceous borders, the natural beauty of 30 acres (12 hectares) of wildflower meadows, 1000 Hybrid Tea roses and the vibrant colours of dahlias.

Autumn
Autumn in a woodland setting such as Anglesey Abbey brings its own special beauty, not least within the Pilgrims' Lawn, the last area of the garden developed by the 1st Lord Fairhaven before his death. Here the autumnal colours are particularly striking.

Winter
Winter does not diminish the appeal of the gardens. In 1998 the Fairhaven Centenary Walk Winter Garden, created by the National Trust, was opened to celebrate the centenary of Lord Fairhaven's birth. The plants within the garden provide winter colour and scent, while in January carpets of winter aconites and snowdrops, for which Anglesey Abbey is renowned, prosper.

OPPOSITE · Top The Lime Avenue in spring
Bottom The Winter Garden

Right Lord Fairhaven in
Guards uniform

ONE MAN'S VISION

'With patience, single-minded devotion and flawless taste, in an age of war and revolution [Lord Fairhaven] has endowed the England of tomorrow with a landscape garden worthy of her past'.

Sir Arthur Bryant, historian and friend of Lord Fairhaven, 1964

It is difficult, gazing across the meticulously maintained gardens at Anglesey Abbey, to imagine the desolate marsh landscape that once existed here. Nor is it easy to envisage that where the present house rises, there once stood the stone church and domestic buildings of the great medieval priory of the Blessed Virgin and St Nicholas.

Following the destruction of the priory in the 16th century, the buildings fell into ruins, and fish ponds, which once provided carp for the refectory tables, became silted up and were lost. The defensive ditches that encircled and protected the priory also fell into a state of disrepair.

The house at Anglesey Abbey was built in the 17th century, though it has been much altered since then. It incorporates remnants of the priory buildings, which can still be seen today. Within the gardens the former fish ponds and ditches appear as undulations in the ground. In the 19th century, pasture adjoining the gardens was planted with hardwood trees, creating a small area of parkland around the house.

In 1926 this modest estate was purchased by the immensely wealthy Huttleston Broughton (later 1st Lord Fairhaven), grandson of an American oil magnate. The house appealed to Huttleston because of its proximity to the family stud, Newmarket race course and some of the finest partridge shoots in the county.

Immediately, he set about enlarging and remodelling the house, creating what we see today. Initially, he showed little interest in gardening, but in the early 1930s embarked on what is now considered to be one of the finest 20th-century gardens in England. This endeavour would last more than 30 years, and provide Lord Fairhaven with immense pleasure.

Below The house from the South Lawn

A GARDEN OF STATUES

For inspiration, Lord Fairhaven drew on early 18th-century formal gardens, both in this country and on the Continent.

Such gardens, with their avenues of hardwood trees terminated by statuary, were well suited to the flat Fenland landscape which Anglesey offered. The poor, often-waterlogged nature of the soil was not so accommodating.

A key element of any formal garden is statuary. Here Lord Fairhaven was greatly helped by the dire economic state of many of England's great country houses, the contents of which were being disposed of at an alarming rate. But one man's poison was to be another man's meat, and in the ensuing years Lord Fairhaven amassed one of the finest collections of garden statuary in the country.

Generally, Lord Fairhaven's taste in sculpture was conservative. He chose mythological and biblical subjects and ornaments rich in classical motifs. The garden statues came from far and near and from many well-known houses and gardens, including Stowe in Buckinghamshire, which is now also owned by the National Trust.

Left A 19th-century bronze copy of an antique marble statue of the hunter goddess Diana

OPPOSITE

Top The Coronation Avenue was planted in 1937 to celebrate the coronation of George VI

Bottom The statue of Meleager and Atalanta on the Olympian Walk

MAKING THE GARDEN

To assist him in achieving his informed and well-thought-out vision for the garden, Lord Fairhaven worked with three successive head gardeners: Walter Grayston, Noel Ayres (who lived for Anglesey) and Noel's son Richard, who continued to work in the gardens after Lord Fairhaven's death in 1966.

Above Lord Fairhaven with his head gardener Noel Ayres

Lord Fairhaven also received horticultural guidance from Major Vernon Daniels, a close friend who provided planting plans for a number of local gardens. Rarity was not important to Lord Fairhaven. He loved indigenous plants, choosing varieties for their colour, form and ability to thrive in the alkaline soil of the garden.

Also unusual was Lord Fairhaven's belief that the planting within the numerous discrete garden enclosures at Anglesey did not have to be at its best throughout the growing season. Instead, he would escort his guests to areas where the floral displays were at their seasonal height.

In the early years, labour from the estate farm was employed to clear and level the land and set out the basic structure of the garden. In all, four gardeners (today there are six) laboured to create and maintain the gardens to the extremely high standard Lord Fairhaven demanded. On occasions, additional help would be available in the form of Lord Fairhaven himself, who would put on his 'leggings and gauntlets' for a 'gardening day' working side-by-side with his men.

OPPOSITE

Top The Anglesey garden team and their equipment

Below Staking out the dahlias and clipping the lawn edges

WILDLIFE IN THE GARDEN

Gardens have an enormous potential to act as nature reserves, and this is especially true for the large gardens of Anglesey Abbey. The recognition of the importance of these gardens for wildlife and the Trust's 'greener' approach to gardening has brought about some management changes in the 21st century.

You may now notice that some grassy areas away from the formal gardens are left unmown until late summer, such as in the South Park, Glade and Meadows (areas 20, 21, 22, 26). This allows the wildflowers to bloom and provide food for butterflies, hoverflies and bees. After the grass has been cut, it is allowed to dry and then is picked up by a mini-baler and taken away to be composted. This new management has been so successful that 50 species of wildflowers have been seen in these meadows, including such special plants as Pyramidal Orchid, Bee Orchid, Spotted Orchid and the rare, tiny Adderstongue Fern. There are also 22 species of wild grasses. Few of these species would have been seen had these areas been mown every fortnight, as in the past. Sinuous paths take you through the long grass so you can enjoy the wildflowers.

Opposite, clockwise from top right A hairy dragonfly, Pyramidal Orchids and a toad

Right A grass snake

Another change is that the use of chemicals has been greatly reduced, and efforts have been made to encourage natural predators of garden pests. Bird boxes encourage insect-eating birds. Deadwood and leaf-piles are left where possible to provide habitats for predatory insects, such as ground beetles, lacewings and ladybirds, that will eat caterpillars and aphids. The results are very encouraging, as 24 species of butterflies thrive in the gardens, 70 species of hoverflies and huge numbers of beetles, grasshoppers and crickets.

The new, larger compost areas have also greatly benefited the grass snakes at Anglesey Abbey, who lay their eggs in the warm rotting vegetation and hide there on cold nights. The main prey for grass snakes are frogs, which breed in the ponds and ditches, and hunt for their own prey, insects and slugs, in the tall grass of the meadows and amongst the flower beds. Thus the key to a healthy garden with thriving wildlife is making sure the connections of the food chain are there from plants to herbivores to predators. At Anglesey Abbey, top of the food chain are the resident tawny owls, sparrowhawks and kestrels.

The Trust is committed to conserving the natural environment, and these changes in practice are intended to create more wildlife-friendly habitats without detracting from the spirit of the 1st Lord Fairhaven's intentions.

LORD FAIRHAVEN'S GARDEN, 1930–45

In the late 1920s Lord Fairhaven began to plant shelter belts around the Anglesey estate to provide privacy and to protect any future planting from the harsh winds that sweep across the fens. By 1930 he was ready to begin work in the gardens proper.

THE JUBILEE AVENUE (24)

The year 1930 coincided with the 800th anniversary of the founding of Anglesey Priory, an event which Lord Fairhaven felt should be commemorated. Consequently, at the end of an avenue of old elm trees known as the Daffodil Walk he placed a large stone urn.

Below The Jubilee Avenue looking north

The plinth on which the urn stands is decorated with Lord Fairhaven's coat of arms and carries an inscription which records the anniversary of the founding of the priory.

The urn was the first commemorative structure Lord Fairhaven introduced into the gardens. It would not be the last. In the years to come, he would create a number of features within the garden to mark important contemporary historical events.

Tragically, the elms in the Daffodil Walk had to be felled in the 1970s after contracting Dutch elm disease. Later, hornbeams were planted in their place. Around 4000 trees within the garden were felled as a result of disease. The planting of the hornbeams coincided with the Silver Jubilee of HM Queen Elizabeth II in 1977, when the avenue was renamed the Jubilee Avenue.

THE ARBORETUM (11)

The first major planting scheme Lord Fairhaven undertook at Anglesey was the Arboretum or woodland garden, which he created within the 19th-century parkland that lay near to the house.

In itself, the creation of an arboretum is not surprising, particularly since Lord Fairhaven had a passion for trees. What is unusual is that he selected trees, some of which are flowering varieties, for their beauty, rather than rarity or scientific value, as is usually the case in an arboretum.

Within the Arboretum, Algerian oak, Japanese hop hornbeam and maidenhair trees were planted, and the lawn was infused with a mixture of snowdrops and golden aconites. The flowering trees include a pink Indian horse chestnut, a Scarlet oak, a tulip and several Judas trees. The branches of the trees in the Arboretum were allowed to grow down to the ground, giving a natural, unmanaged look. This approach was prompted not only by Lord Fairhaven's desire to create an area of informality, but also by his belief that trees should not be needlessly cut back. Whenever he saw the severed branches of trees, he would question the gardeners as to the reason for felling. Woe betide the gardener who did not have an adequate reason for severing the branch!

Below The Arboretum

LODE MILL (7)

In 1934 Lord Fairhaven purchased a derelict cement factory which stood next to the gardens. Much of the complex was demolished, though an 18th-century water-powered mill, Lode Mill, which probably stood on the site of a monastic mill, was retained.

Formerly a corn mill, Lode Mill was modified about 1900 to grind the raw ingredients, mainly limestone, needed for cement production. The limestone was then burned in a kiln, producing cement clinker. This was returned to the mill and ground to a fine powder. Shortly after acquiring the mill, Lord Fairhaven, appreciating its charm and historical value, restored the building as a functional, yet attractive, feature of the garden. Flour production was resumed in 1982 following the restoration of the mill to working order by the Cambridgeshire Wind and Watermill Society.

THE QUARRY POOL (8)

A further relic of the industrial age, Quarry Pool, a flooded coprolite pit, lies close to the mill. Coprolite (fossilised dinosaur dung) was used as a fertiliser in the 19th century and was found extensively in this area of East Anglia. A railway was constructed from the quarry to convey the coprolite to the mill, where it was ground to powder.

Above The Quarry Pool
Opposite Bottisham Lode and Lode Mill

THE CORONATION AVENUE (27) AND THE CROSS AVENUE (28)

Having repaired Lode Mill, Lord Fairhaven embarked, from 1937 onwards, on the planting of the Coronation Avenue, the Cross Avenue and the Warriors' Walk. These avenues, an essential element of any formal garden, provide shade for those venturing outdoors and framed the distant views of the sculpture that terminates them.

Below The Coronation Avenue

The Coronation Avenue of chestnut trees celebrates the enthronement of George VI. At the entrance to the avenue Lord Fairhaven erected two massive stone piers, each surmounted by a *lead sphinx* of mid-18th-century origin. They are probably by John Cheere, a leading maker of cast-lead statues in 18th-century England.

At the junction of the Coronation Avenue and the Cross Avenue, Lord Fairhaven placed *six statues of caryatids*, female figures which in Greek architecture were used as an alternative to columns. The Anglesey caryatids were made in 1793 of Coade Stone (fired clay produced at the London factory of a Mrs Emily Coade). Originally, they stood in the entrance hall of Buckingham House, London.

Lord Fairhaven planned to terminate the Coronation Avenue with an eye-catching Gothic folly, which was to be placed in the fields beyond the garden. Sadly, he did not fulfil this ambition.

THE WARRIORS' WALK (4)

Unusually, the Warriors' Walk was planted with Norway spruce and larch, of which Lord Fairhaven was very fond. The walk takes its name from a ship's figurehead, carved in timber, which was placed at the end of the avenue. The figurehead, once brightly coloured, formerly adorned the prow of HMS *Warrior*, the first iron-clad warship in the Royal Navy (now on show in Portsmouth Historic Dockyard). A figurehead taken from HMS *Hector*, again of timber, was placed at the opposite end of the walk.

By the 1960s the figureheads, now painted grey, had decayed beyond repair and were removed from the garden. This pleased the 3rd Lord Fairhaven, who as a child had been afraid of the statues. He was amused later to learn that the then Head Gardener, Richard Ayres, also found the figures disconcerting.

Above The Cross Avenue

Left An 18th-century stone herm on Warriors' Walk

THE FORMAL GARDEN (19)

In addition to the formal avenues, in the mid-1930s Lord Fairhaven began creating a number of enclosed flower gardens.

The Formal Garden, the first of these features, demonstrated Lord Fairhaven's belief that a garden could be planted with a single species of flowers, which would bloom for a short period (in this case spring) and be visited only at this time. Hyacinths of pink and white or pale yellow and white were planted, but Lord Fairhaven did not find the combination pleasing, and they were replaced with blue and white hues. Four thousand hyacinth bulbs were planted and renewed every three years. Lord Fairhaven particularly enjoyed visiting the Formal Garden at dusk or dawn, when the flowers, 'wet with dew, produced a heady scent'. Lord Fairhaven introduced dahlia cultivars, in shades of red and yellow, to provide autumn colour.

Within the Formal Garden Lord Fairhaven placed *four bronze urns*, 19th-century copies of originals designed for the gardens of Versailles by Claude Ballin, goldsmith to Louis XIV. A *stone statue of Father Time*, English, *c.*1700, and formerly at Stowe, also stands in the garden.

Right Father Time in the Formal Garden

OPPOSITE

Top The Formal Garden

Bottom *Dahlia* 'Hillcrest Desire'

THE DAHLIA GARDEN (16)

A further flower area, the Dahlia Garden, was – unusually for Lord Fairhaven – planted to provide floral interest throughout the year. Deep blue forget-me-nots and a combination of yellow or scarlet tulips supplied early colour. The forget-me-nots and tulips were lifted after flowering and replaced with dahlias for late summer colour.

This garden no longer has a spring display. Due to the milder winters, the dahlias continue to flower until mid- to late November, by which time it is too late to plant young spring bedding.

At the entrance to the Dahlia Garden stands a *pair of stone griffins* (Dresden, 1730). Within stands a *marble statue of Apollino* (Italian, *c.*1800), the adolescent Apollo, who was associated in Roman mythology with the sun. After the Second World War a stone plinth, on which stands a *bronze statue of a faun*, was inscribed with the text 'Annus mirabilis – 1945'.

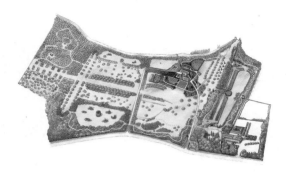

Opposite Statue of a satyr blowing on a conch shell at the entrance to the Rose Garden

THE ROSE GARDEN (18)

In 1939 Lord Fairhaven created the Rose Garden, a quintessentially English feature. The Rose Garden produces spectacular colour and scent in the summer months, and is a far cry from the dilapidated greenhouses, weed-ridden paths and abandoned vegetable and flower borders that existed when Lord Fairhaven acquired Anglesey.

Below The Rose Garden

Forty beds were dug, each planted with a different variety of rose – in all, some 1000 bushes. Lord Fairhaven, ever conscious of the needs of his plants, replaced the poor-quality earth in the garden with loam. Today, two or three beds are dug up annually, the soil is changed, and new varieties of rose are planted.

Ultimately, Lord Fairhaven placed early 18th-century **lead statues of Apollo and Diana**, and a 19th-century **bronze copy of Donatello's David**, within the garden. Without doubt, the finest sculptures within the Rose Garden are **four marble vases** by the eminent sculptors Laurent Delvaux and Peter Scheemakers. They date from the late 1720s and were made for the long-demolished Wanstead House in Essex.

In order to prevent further decay of the fragile marble surfaces, the vases were removed from the garden in 2006, and the present replicas introduced. The originals are currently on display in the new British Sculpture galleries of the Victoria & Albert Museum in London.

At the time the Rose Garden was being created, changes were made to the maintenance regimes within the woodland areas of the garden. These were made possible by the introduction of a tractor-towed mechanical mower. Prior to this, the large expanses of grass within the garden were left long, and paths were cut through in the traditional manner, using scythes. Following the introduction of the mower, the gardens assumed a managed appearance, though long grass was maintained immediately below the trees. Lord Fairhaven encouraged wildflowers to grow here, which he thought provided as striking and reliable a floral display as any well-tended cultivated bloom.

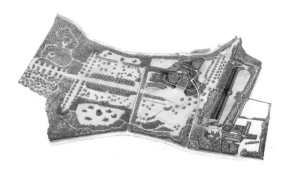

LORD FAIRHAVEN'S GARDEN, 1945–66

Following the trauma of the Second World War, Lord Fairhaven made ready to progress work within his beloved gardens.

THE EMPERORS' WALK (5)

One of the earliest post-war undertakings was the creation of the Emperors' Walk, a formal avenue of Norway spruce and larch, which runs parallel to the Warriors' Walk. At opposite ends of the walk he placed *bronze statues of the hunter goddess Diana and the demi-god Silenus carrying the infant Bacchus*. Along the avenue he erected *twelve marble busts of Roman emperors*, from which the walk takes its name.

Right Bust of a Roman emperor on the Emperors' Walk

OPPOSITE

Top The Pagoda

Bottom The circular copper beech hedge encloses lead figures from Stowe landscape garden

Having planted the Emperors' Walk, Lord Fairhaven erected the Pagoda, purchased from an architectural salvage company, on a cross path between the Warriors' and Emperors' Walks. In addition to providing interest and surprise, the Pagoda had a practical purpose, giving protection to an ancient Roman *porphyry tazza* (or bowl), which Lord Fairhaven placed inside.

Nearby Lord Fairhaven planted a copper beech hedge, circular in plan, which he adorned with *four lead figures* that once surmounted the pediment of the Temple of Concord and Victory at Stowe. Two of the figures represent the arts of painting and sculpture; that which bears a caste mark on its forehead may represent Asia.

In 1979 a storm wrought havoc on the Warriors' and Emperors' Walks, toppling the trees like ninepins. The few that remained standing were felled, and the avenues replanted with spruce and yew.

Below Statue of the Saxon
God Tiw by Michael Rysbrack

THE HERBACEOUS GARDEN (15)

By the early 1950s, Lord Fairhaven turned his attention to the creation of a further flower compartment, known as the Herbaceous Garden. It was laid out in what had been an ornamental vegetable and flower garden.

The curvilinear shape of the garden was defined with beech hedges. Lord Fairhaven designed the garden to be viewed in the summer months. In June irises, lupins and pyrethrums bloom, giving way in July to delphiniums, lilies, thalictrums, heleniums, achilleas and blue salvias.

The way Lord Fairhaven grouped the plants within the Herbaceous Garden was considered unusual at the time, with large clumps of single varieties being placed for their shape and form rather than (as was more normal at the time) in blocks of colour. Nor were bush roses and shrubs used, as was also common. Major Daniels, ever-practical, introduced palmate-leaved rodgersias and glaucous hostas within the herbaceous borders at the entrance to the garden, where shade predominates.

Remarkably, the borders within the Herbaceous Garden have never been replanted, though varieties which have not thrived have

Above *Geranium grandiflora* in the Herbaceous Garden

Below Delphiniums, foxgloves and salvias in the Herbaceous Garden

been changed. Perhaps the greatest achievement of the Herbaceous Garden is that its natural appearance belies the efforts, particularly in staking-out, that go into its maintenance.

The leading 18th-century sculptor Michael Rysbrack carved the ***stone statue of the Saxon God Tiw*** which stands at the centre of the Herbaceous Garden. The effigy of Tiw, from which we get the word Tuesday, came from Stowe.

THE TEMPLE LAWN (25)

The coronation of HM Queen Elizabeth in 1953 provided Lord Fairhaven with the opportunity to create yet another commemorative area, the Temple and the Temple Lawn.

The Temple is perhaps the most spectacular, and certainly the most monumental, structure within the gardens at Anglesey. It is very different in character from, but just as grand as, the Coronation Avenue, which had been planted to mark the enthronement of the Queen's father.

The site chosen for the Temple was an uninspiring hayfield known as the Six Acre – 'uneven, spongy and wet'. However, Lord Fairhaven felt the area had some promise and worked with its pleasantly irregular shape and the mature shelterbelt of beech, elms, alders, sycamores and willows which encompassed it.

Below The Temple

The Temple, which was erected in this sheltered spot, was conceived as a great sculptural essay rather than an architectural structure.

Considerable thought was given as to the position of the Temple within the field. It was placed in such a way that glimpses of it could be seen from outside the planting which encircled it. When the Temple was viewed from a distance, the observer would be tempted to investigate.

Massive concrete foundations were required to support the columns that define the Temple. Each column, which weighs two tons, was lifted into place using only block and tackle. The columns formerly stood at the entrance to Lord Chesterfield's London house, which was demolished in 1937.

At the entrance to the Temple two early 18th-century *lead statues of lions* by the Dutch sculptor Jan Van Nost the elder stand guard. Within the Temple Lord Fairhaven placed an early 20th-century *marble statue of David* readying his sling to slay the giant Goliath. It was copied from the 17th-century original by the great Italian Baroque sculptor Bernini.

Planting also plays an important role within the Temple Lawn, where three island beds, one with colours of grey and gold and two of strong reds and purples, provide colour in summer and winter alike. Elders, willows, poplars, plums, rhus and buckthorns vie for space in the densely planted beds, where effect is dependent on mass rather than the appearance of individual trees and shrubs.

THE PINETUM (1)

Lord Fairhaven continued to create new areas of interest within the gardens almost until his death in 1966. In 1953 he planted the Pinetum, a collection of specimen coniferous trees which include *Pinus strobus* and *Picea omerika*. The National Trust continues to add to and enhance this area.

THE PILGRIMS' LAWN (30)

Lord Fairhaven's last major project was the creation of the Pilgrims' Lawn. As with the Temple Lawn created over ten years previously, he planted island beds with shrubs and trees, including tall conifers such as *Leylandii*. Strong yellow and purple colouring predominates, particularly in autumn, when the islands are designed to be at their most brilliant. A 19th-century *stone figure of a pilgrim* provides the garden with its name. Sadly, Lord Fairhaven would not live to see the garden in all its glory. It was completed in 1967.

Left The entrance to the Pinetum

Below *Cotoneaster salicifolia* on Pilgrims' Lawn

THE NATIONAL TRUST

THE WINTER GARDEN (2)

The Winter Garden has been one of the most significant and popular developments within these gardens since the National Trust took over their management. It provides a fine memorial to the 1st Lord Fairhaven and is just the thing to lift the spirits during the long months of winter.

History

The Winter Garden was opened in November 1998 as part of the celebrations of the centenary of the birth of the 1st Lord Fairhaven. The idea for a winter garden came originally from John Sales (then the National Trust's Head of Gardens) and Richard Ayres (at that time Head Gardener of Anglesey Abbey). The initial plan for the garden was drawn up by John Sales, and planting began during spring of 1998.

The site chosen, on the eastern boundary of the estate, had previously been planted with quick-growing conifers to provide shelter belts for the gardens. These had outgrown their useful life and were removed during the 1990s.

The first stage in creating the Winter Garden was to plant the eastern edge of the East Lawn with a line of *Acer negundo* (Box Elder) and a mixed planting of *Cornus mas* (Cornelian Cherry) and *Prunus subhirtella* 'Autumnalis' (Autumn Cherry), all chosen for their winter colour. A central half-circle of *Tilia petiolaris* (Weeping Lime), one of Lord Fairhaven's favourite trees, was created at the same time.

Once the framework had been established, the path could be laid and the planting of the extensive bedding areas undertaken. The path is some 450m long, and the garden is about a hectare (2.5 acres) in size. It contains more than 150 different varieties of plants.

OPPOSITE

Left *Cornus alba* and *Rubus tibetianus* 'Silver Fern' in the Winter Garden

Right Ornamental grasses in the Winter Garden

A journey through the Winter Garden
On leaving the reception area and bearing right, you walk through a young plantation of *Sequoia giganteum* (Giant Redwood) before joining the serpentine gravel pathway that weaves and twists the length of the garden. The garden is long and narrow so the meandering path allows new surprises on every bend. After the first corner you come upon an array of colours produced by many stems, which were chosen to be at their best in the winter months, when bright flowers are in short supply. *Salix alba* 'Britzensis' (Scarlet Willow), *Cornus alba* 'Westonbirt' (Red-barked Dogwood) and *Rubus tibetianus* 'Silver Fern' (a form of bramble) glow orange, dazzling red and pure white respectively. The path winds through a stand of the fire-like stems of *Cornus sanguinea* 'Midwinter Fire' (a variety of the Common Dogwood).

Below
Narcissus 'February Gold'

It is not only through the eyes that pleasure is found. The air is full of the scent of Sarcococca (Christmas Box), Viburnum, Chimonanthus (Winter Sweet), Mahonia and the very sweet perfume of winter-flowering honeysuckle (*Lonicera standishii*). The sense of touch is engaged by the polished bark of *Prunus serrula* (Tibetan Cherry), which cries out to be stroked (and is reachable from the path).

At the half-way point a circular hedge of *Elaeagnus ebbingeii* creates a quiet area to sit and enjoy the simple and soothing planting of grasses, to listen to their rustling in the breeze and, during the autumn months, to enjoy the scent from the flowers of the hedge. The statue in the centre is a copy of a 19th-century bronze held elsewhere in the abbey. It is of a nude youth with raised arms, and is stamped 'F Barbedienne, Fondeur'. The plaque on the plinth celebrates the centenary of the birth of Huttleston Broughton, 1st Lord Fairhaven.

Many types of ground cover have been used along the route, including Bergenia, Hedera (Ivy), Euonymus, Luzula (Woodrush), Vinca (Periwinkle) and Pulmonaria. There are thousands of spring flowers and bulbs such as Galanthus (Snowdrop), Crocus, Tulip, Iris and many types of Hellebore. Throughout the garden strongly contrasting colours of foliage have been planted to grab the attention, and many of the shrubs and trees still (birds permitting) have their berries and fruits to add to the colour.

Good use of trees with special winter interest can be seen everywhere. Particularly fine examples are *Arbutus unedo* (Killarney Strawberry Tree) that displays its strawberry-like fruit in the weeks before Christmas; many snake-barked maples (*Acer pensylvanicum*, davidii and *tegmentosum*); the twisted twigs of *Corylus avellana* 'Contorta' (Twisted Hazel); and the grand finale of the whole Winter Garden, which is a grove of the pure white trunks of *Betula utilis* var *jacquemontii* (Himalayan Silver Birch) dramatically rising from a deep red underplanting of *Bergenia* 'Bressingham Ruby'.

Winter gardening takes full advantage of the low levels of the sun. So on your way round, notice how the sun shines through the red thorns of *Rosa sericea* ssp *omeiensis pteracantha* and picks out the prickly stems of *Rubus phoenicolasius* and any trees with flaking bark such as *Prunus serrula* and *Acer griseum* (Paper Bark Maple).

On leaving the Winter Garden, the path continues through wooded areas full of snowdrops and aconites towards Lode Mill.

Below Winter-flowering *Viburnum bodnantense* 'Dawn'

THE WOODLAND PATH (10)

The Woodland Path, which was cut through a shelter belt of mixed deciduous and box bushes in 2004, was opened the same year. With the help of children from local schools, the garden team laid out the pathway and added boxes for birds and for over-wintering flying insects such as bumble bees. Piles of brush and logs were left to provide 'hedgehog hotels' and cover for ground insects and small mammals. Another group of children devised an illustrated guide to the area.

This meandering path has been underplanted with thousands of snowdrops to give an additional area for viewing these wonderful plants, which have been given ideal conditions in which to thrive. The dappled light and fertile soil of the woodland floor is ideal to establish these. Varieties such as *Galanthus nivalis* cultivars, along with many cultivars of *Galanthus elwesii*, can be found here.

On a fine early spring day it lifts the spirit to wander through this area – white and green of the snowdrops at your feet, and shafts of brilliant gold from the sun shining through the open canopy.

Left Snowdrops in spring

Opposite *Galanthus* 'Wendy's Gold'

MAINTAINING STANDARDS

Working with the current Lord Fairhaven, the National Trust continues to maintain the standards set by the 1st Lord. Mechanical mowers, hedge-trimmers and powerful blowers, which remove the tons of leaves that fall annually, all contribute toward this endeavour. Ultimately, it is dedication and hard physical work that achieve such standards.

Challenges for the future

Managing a great garden such as Anglesey has its challenges. Rain-borne acids have eroded some of the garden sculptures, which have had to be housed indoors to protect their delicate detail. The Trust has replaced them with high-quality replicas in order to preserve the views designed by Lord Fairhaven.

The fact that Anglesey lies in one of the driest regions of Britain has encouraged the garden team to adopt a comprehensive approach to recycling green waste. In time, it will be returned to the garden as compost, assisting in water retention, reducing pollution from burning, and adding nutrients to the soil. We are proud that we now recycle around 95 per cent of all garden waste, and encourage others to do the same.

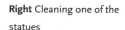

Right Cleaning one of the statues